To

_____

From

_____

Date

_____

THE
LEADERS'
LADDER
WITH
R.E.A.D

Proven Principles for Leadership Excellence

THE
CORNERSTONE
P U B L I S H I N G

BOSEDE ADETUNJI

THE LEADERS' LADDER WITH R.E.A.D

Proven Principles for Leadership Excellence

Copyright © 2018 by Bosede Adetunji
ISBN: 978-1732001732

A Publication of Lily in His Hands LLC.

Published by
Cornerstone Publishing
A Division of Cornerstone Creativity Group LLC
Phone: +1(516) 547-4999
info@thecornerstonepublishers.com
www.thecornerstonepublishers.com

To order bulk copies of this book or to contact the author please call Lily in His Hands, LLC @
+1 (614) 596-4626

www.lilyinhishands.com | www.bosedeadetunji.com

FOREWORD

Leadership has been simply defined as INFLUENCE by renowned author and leadership expert, John Maxwell. Of course, when amplified this can mean a lot of things as you will discover in this book. Our effectiveness at anything we do is determined by our leadership ability. Everyone therefore that will ever taste the grapes of success will have to commit their lives to a life-long study of this amazing subject. That is why Bosede Adetunji's contribution to the body of knowledge is most welcome. With a vast world made up of different nationalities, backgrounds and perspectives, as many expositions of a subject as important as leadership cannot be overemphasized so as many people as possible can understand it. Raised in Africa and at a time when the feminine gender was still struggling to find her voice, she relocated to a more liberated world and then responded to a divine calling to lead men and women.

After defining the subject, the author enunciates ageless principles that further affirm the assertion that 'Success is predictable'. The God of the universe has designed His creation to be governed by eternal and unchangeable principles. As the burden of leadership came to rest upon the shoulders of Joshua, the task must have overwhelmed and intimidated him. Who can fill the shoes of Moses? Who can lead a nation that Moses himself could not take into the promised land? In the midst of his anxiety comes the voice of God;

"This Book of the Law shall not depart from your mouth, but you shall meditate in it day and night, that you may observe to do according to all that is written in it. For then you will make your way prosperous, and then you will have good success." Joshua 1:8 NKJV

The key was delivered to him. It was to make the Word of God His Leadership manual, his guide and closest ally. There he will discover God's Law which included hundreds of spiritual, moral and environmental principles for nation building. Today with the Bible including the Law, the prophets, the gospels and the epistles supported by a wide body of knowledge on bookshelves and on electronic platforms, there has never being a greater opportunity to succeed at leadership. If we seek to know, understand and practice the principles, we will succeed. The author expatiates on the most fundamental of these principles and after exalting the value of leadership, simplifies the mountain by reducing it to a plain through practical applicable wisdom.

You will see more clearly, journey faster and work smarter after reading this beautiful book, LEADER'S LADDER WITH R.E.A.D.

Victor Adeyemi
Senior Pastor
Global Harvest church
April 2018

DEDICATION

Jesus Christ, You, alone deserve all praise for being the only Leader that is worthy to emulate. Singing:

…YOU came from heaven to earth, to show the way
From the earth to the cross, my life to stay
From the cross to the grave
From the grave to the sky
Lord I lift your name up high.

Jesus Christ came to teach ALL the principles of Leadership we can ever think of. He also showed examples on how to lead, through the Servant-Leadership formats. And left indelible footprints of a true leader of influence.

Lord Jesus Christ, I dedicate this to YOU, be honored and be praised.

ACKNOWLEDGMENTS

All thanks to you, my only WWW. HUSBAND. WE, Pastor Amos Olufemi Adetunji, I salute your swift nudges and cool pushes that makes the leadership prowess in me to be refined.

Leading the people of God at the congregation standpoint was huge, I almost ran away, but you helped me to develop the principles in this book.

I appreciate all my Christ Harvest Church Family, especially, all that started the vision with us, and still believe God through us, (I wish I could mention names). I love you all.

To all that I have been a mentee to, all my leaders in ministry and secular world, thank you so much for all the seeds you have consciously and unconsciously planted in me.

Rev. Victor Adeyemi, of Global Harvest

Church, I salute you and the heart of leadership you possess. Thank you for your supports.

Also, to you my brothers, you all, never knew the giant you were sculpturing into me through your masculinity traits I went through in ages past, they are all in any ways culminated to the leader I become today…THE ELUJOBAS = Bishop Ola, Engr. Olalekan, Engr. Omotayo, Chief Acct. Olayinka, Engr. Olakunle (and your wives and children) this is for all of you. I LOVE YOU ALL

CONTENTS

INTRODUCTION

The subject of leadership is not entirely new. Virtually everyone has an idea of who a leader is or should be. A leader is:

A person who holds a dominant or superior position in a field, and is able to exercise a high degree of control or influence over others.

The one in charge; the person who convinces other people to follow. A great leader inspires confidence in other people and moves them to action.

Anyone who influences the thinking, development or actions of others toward a course/path in order to get to tangible goal(s). This may be a parent, a sibling, a friend, a coach, a CEO, or any other person.

What the above reveals is that a leader is

that person who occupies a dominant or superior position, is in charge or in control, and is able to influence the thinking, action or development of others. However, after carefully analyzing a series of data and case studies, I have come to know that the efficiency of a leader is not contained in definitions but in the functions of the leadership office. This is why many communities and organizations are continuously yearning for a better leader, every now and then.

In most countries of the world, especially those in the "third world", there is often a dearth of good leadership, despite general knowledge of who a good leader should be. In other words, while it may be the case that some people assume leadership positions without knowledge of what is expected of them, the majority at least have an idea of who a good leader is or the character he should possess; yet, once these same people get into office, to the pinnacle of the hierarchy, they begin to thrust bitter pills into their followers' mouths.

Here is a graphical outline of the qualities that most people expect of a good leader:

I'm sure you would agree with me that these

attributes are basic and not in any way extreme. But, then, if we admit that these qualities are essential and indispensable, why are many businesses, organizations, churches and groups filled with embittered and demoralized followers? Why are the tenures of many leaders filled with complaints and why do they leave many people dissatisfied even after their exit from office? Or to put it more directly, why is the application of the above principles so difficult to practice? If we know who a good leader is, why do people get to the top of the ladder and begin to operate otherwise?

This book examines leadership in all spheres of life – political leadership, organizational leadership, spiritual leadership and so on. Getting into a leadership position is good, but becoming a leader is far better. It is therefore a demonstration of wisdom to seek to become a leader with productive potentials, someone who has values to maintain structures, someone known to be an agent of positive change to his circles of influence and community at large.

I believe that as we take a ride through the principles of R-E-A-D, as analyzed in this book, we will not only have a fulfilling tenure of office as great leaders but also leave footprints of profound legacies and indelible impacts that will reverberate among the people for a long time to come.

Chapter 1

LEADERSHIP REVISITED

"If your actions inspire others to dream more, learn more, do more and become more, you are a leader."
~ John Quincy Adams

In contemporary times, leadership has become such a poignant concept as to have different interpretations - some constructive, others destructive. Perception of leadership also has a lot to do with experience and environment. To people in certain parts of the world, leadership is not often an appealing concept. The reason is because among the politicians in many of these countries, leadership is the ability to manipulate people in order to gain or retain power and enrich themselves. And the continuum seems never-ending, from one politician to the other. Unsurprisingly, their citizens are often disappointed and disillusioned, wondering how an incumbent was voted or allowed into office in the first place.

Still on the wrong perception of leadership - to some people, leadership in the marketplace or in business operations is the ability to greedily make quick money at the expense of others, without minding who or what is affected. If you happen to be trying to follow the rules and ethics of a business, such would tell you that there are faster ways of making it. They would also tell you that it's only the slow ones that are caught, and that you won't have followers if you are too slow.

In many homes also, leadership is misconceived as how well a father (or both parents) can pull and push around his family in an authoritative manner. Until he gets older and realizes that the damage he has done in his family is irreversible.

Religious circles are not left out of the misconceptions attached to leadership. Leadership is often seen as how well spiritual leaders can manipulatively hypnotize their members to do and undo "church" for the benefits of their pockets and families. To these people, "miracle" is everything, and it can take all forms, from the farcical to the magical to the utterly diabolical. The excuse of such religious "leaders" is that the society would not reckon with them if their congregations cannot be hypnotized to see their so-called miracles and prophecies. Their ultimate purpose, of course, is to generate increase in size and spread of their church branches – which will mean more money and popularity for them.

While I really don't want to dwell too much on these erroneous perceptions of leadership in this book, I must quickly emphasize that one of the many truths that religious people, especially church leaders, fail to realize is that church is God's property and not theirs. Moreover, Jesus, our pacesetter, mostly demonstrated miracles to strengthen those who were weak in faith. John 4:47-48 says, "When he heard that Jesus had come out of Judea into Galilee, he went to Him and implored Him to come down and heal his son, for he was at the point of death. Then Jesus said to him, "Unless you people see signs and wonders, you will by no means believe."

Jesus, here, was referring to those outside of the faith, who needed to see signs and wonders before they believed the word of God. Note that the "these people" did not include the disciples, because they were members of the "inner circle" with Christ. Jesus spent more of His time with the disciples teaching and building them up with the Word, not demonstrating miracles to them. Our churches are like this inner circle. Ironically, rather than doing what Jesus did - edifying and teaching people with the sound doctrine of the Word, which is God Himself – what many church leaders focus on is miracles. What they are unknowingly implying is that their congregations comprise the sick and unbelievers, which in itself does not speak well of their ministries.

Jesus came to perfect all areas of the gospel; but church leaders nowadays are fixated on hypnotic miracles. This is a reason many churches are in shambles spiritually – the leadership has become more or less disconnected from God.

DEFINITIONS AND BEYOND

In a simple way, dictionary.com defines leadership as:

- the position or function of a leader, a person who guides or directs a group.

- ability to lead.

- an act or instance of leading; guidance; direction.

- the leaders of a group.

The above descriptions illustrate, in a nutshell, the importance of having the position of leadership occupied by someone who is strong, confident and possesses the agility of a go-getter. The leader is not just leading himself or his household, but a group (a community) of people whose lives and destinies can be made or marred within the duration of his leadership, depending on the style of operation he adopts.

Let me point out however that my intention in this book is not to bring out the best definition of leadership or to enumerate the qualities of a good leader. These have been explored and explained by so many great writers, speakers and teachers. My main concern is, why is there so much deficiency in the perception and practice of leadership all around us? Does it mean that people who assume leadership positions don't have access to the many published principles of leadership? Or maybe they know all about the principles but simply choose not to put them into action.

With reference to available insights on leadership, it is worthy to note that leadership styles are defined in relation to their operations and influences. Osmond Vitez has, for instance, identified three forms of leadership in the business world. According to him: "Three types of leadership are common in business: authoritarian, democratic and laissez-faire. Authoritarian leadership is commanding and sets clear expectations for employees in the organizational. Democratic leadership encourages feedback and input from managers or employees regarding organizational performance. Laissez-faire is a hands-off approach, where managers and employees work according to their own preference and schedule."

Rose Johnson, on the other hand, has identified five styles of leadership, namely: laissez-faire; autocratic; participative; transactional and transformational. Ahmed Raza exceeded this list when he wrote an article featuring twelve leadership styles. They are: autocratic; democratic; strategic; transformational; team; cross-cultural; facilitative; laissez-faire; transactional; coaching; charismatic; and visionary leadership styles.

Regardless of their variations, what all these definitions and many others reveal is that there is indeed a vast array of resources to guide the operations of leadership towards making positive impacts on individuals and organizations. What has been discovered however is that the more the styles proffered by leadership experts and strategists, the more stunted organizations and businesses become and the more disappointed the followers are. The letdowns, notwithstanding, society cannot do without a leader - a true, functional one.

NECESSITY OF LEADERSHIP

For our communities and organizations to be orderly, progressive and prosperous, there's need for a functional leader. The influence of a leader in an organization, whether secular or spiritual, cannot be overestimated. A society cannot have a unified front or a strong identity without a leader. The numerous possibilities of individual potentials, education, career development, social cohesion and economic empowerment can only be adequately harnessed and maximized by an effective, forward-thinking leader.

At the micro level, a happy family is dependent on an inspiring leader. And since the family forms the bedrock of the nation, such a leader builds a strong nation and a generally happier society. Essentially, therefore, leadership is the most effective tool to ignite passion and inspire action in people, and to achieve a common goal for an organization or a society. If a transformational change is to be achieved in all spheres of life, a charismatic leader cannot be overlooked.

In a nutshell, in order to take the required steps towards achieving a set goal, overcoming obstacles that foster retrogression and birthing revolutionary changes, society at every level needs a leader who is honest, positive-minded, focused, innovative and inspirational. Such will always be remembered to be effective.

Interestingly, researches have shown and writers have claimed that some people are born leaders, while others cultivate the necessary skills. This means that if you have the passion to serve humanity in a leadership position but don't think you possess the natural ability or gift to lead, you can learn the art of leadership and hone it for wide-ranging transformations.

UPSHOTS OF LEADERSHIP FAILURE

The question of leadership often rears up its head each time I look at some societies or nations that are still struggling with growth socially and economically. In thinking of this, the third world nations easily spring to mind. Ironically, many of the countries in this category are endowed with natural resources that can feed and enrich each of the citizens. Unfortunately, however, the distribution of these resources is often fundamentally flawed because of the absence of a good leader. The wealth-sharing formula is either blatantly lopsided or simply geared towards the interests of a few privileged individuals.

As I noted earlier, even in some of the so-called democratic societies in these regions, the dismal picture of leadership is the same. Citizens languish and struggle to meet their needs and fulfill their aspirations, while the elected leaders revel in wanton luxury. Of course, it is in such societies that the middle class is conspicuously absent; that is, you are either up or down; in lower class or upper class; rich or poor. Worse still, your educational attainments or vocational skills have no bearing whatsoever on the position you occupy (especially in public service) because the positions are assigned according to how "connected" you are to the people at the top. So, it would not be surprising to find a zoologist by training heading a bank or a linguist appointed as the managing director of a petroleum corporation.

The ultimate repercussion of leadership absence or failure is, of course, disintegration. I have personally observed that as the consciousness of people continues to be awakened (through mass literacy) and they keep realizing how much of their common wealth is being wasted, mismanaged or embezzled, disintegration is inevitable. Look around, and you would discover that societies and societal structures and institutions are rapidly disintegrating. And if care is not taken, total chaos, better known as anarchy, is to be expected. Some Arab nations recently experienced this (remember Arab Spring?).

A state of anarchy is such in which there is total confusion and breakdown of law and order. This can result from loss of confidence in leadership. When followers have experienced prolonged betrayal by their successive leaders, then disregard for authority and, ultimately, rebellion will definitely follow. People begin to take laws into their hands, because they don't see the point in reposing confidence in an incorrigibly dishonest person or putting their future in jeopardy due to their past experiences with their so-called 'leaders'.

LEADERSHIP PRINCIPLES

Practical leadership is all about principles and strategies. And this is what this book is all about. In a short while, I will be discussing some proven principles of effective leadership which I have coined in the acronym, **R-E-A-D.** These principles, if well applied, will bring spectacular transformations to organizations and communities.

However before then, we need to understand the place of principles in leadership. According to the dictionary, a principle can refer to:

- A moral rule or belief that helps you know

what is right and wrong and that influences your actions.

- A basic truth or theory; an idea that forms the basis of something

- A law or fact of nature that explains how something works or why something happens.

- Fundamental norms, rules, or values that represent what is desirable and positive for a person, group, organization, or community, and help it in determining the rightfulness or wrongfulness of its actions.

Principles are more fundamental than policies and objectives, and are meant to govern both. They act like formats or templates that have been proven to guide someone in achieving a goal. Here are few examples of principles:

- The principle of gravity says that everything that goes up must come down.

- The principle of giving says that the more you give, the more you get. As the scripture states in Ecclesiastes 11:1, "Cast your bread upon the waters, For you will find it after many days."

Albert Einstein too has rightly said, "The value of a man resides in what he gives and NOT in what he is capable of receiving."

POWER OF PRINCIPLES

Let me show you how a principle woks, using the example of giving. There is a story about a billionaire, who was predicted to die within a year due to a rare illness that subjected him to only being able to digest milk and crackers. He started distributing his wealth and assets to hospitals, research efforts and mission work. Little did he know that the cure for his illness would be discovered through the research into a medication (penicillin) which was one of the researches he had financed. Through his application of the principle of giving, he not only got healed but also got to live for a very long time

What I have tried to show you thus far is that principles work and are proven to bring results. Their efficacy cuts across the physical, natural, and spiritual worlds. And the same applies to leadership. Leadership does not only thrive on rules and policies, but also firmly utilizes some principles and strategies for generational effects.

Let's now proceed to explore the principles for exceptional and transformational leadership.

Chapter 2

R - RELIABILITY AND RESPONSIBILITY

"A true leader is someone whose words and actions continued to be used and referred to after that person must have left the leadership" ~ *Myles Munroe*

For someone's words and actions to be a reference resource for success, even after his departure, shows the efficacy and reliability of such a leader. His words must have been tested and proven beyond reasonable doubt. His character must have been very transparent and trusted. Such leadership must have given people so much confidence, based on the consistency of the leader over a period of time.

Reliability has been defined in various ways. It can be seen as "the quality of being trustworthy or of performing consistently well". It can also mean "the degree to which the result of a measurement, calculation or specification can be dependent on to be accurate."

To apply this to leadership, we have to know, first of all, that anyone who influences and guides others is acting in the capacity of a leader, regardless of whether he possesses a corresponding title or not. People within your circle of influence are counting on you to deliver results that will have positive impacts on their lives and livelihoods.

TEST OF RELIABILITY

Reliability is primarily determined by the ability to preserve and project the vision and mission of the organization, group, institution or church that entrusted the leader with the platform on which he is operating. This, of course, will depend on how much knowledge you have about the organization and its purpose of existence, as well as the best means of advancing its cause. Getting and applying this knowledge comes from what you do with the avalanche of resources that you have around you.

The saying is indeed true that "you can only give what you have". If your roots are not consistently tapping into some rich and tested resources from other people that have been on the leadership platform before you or people that have higher levels of grace or experience than you, your leadership will not only end up falling by the wayside like others but your "reliability" status would have been terribly diminished.

To build a solid image of reliability around your leadership, quality of purpose, idea and vision must be your watchword. In other words, you must make all you do to bear the trademark of quality and excellence – and you must be consistent about this. This is the seed that is going to be tested and proven for its genuineness before people can put their trust in you. This consistent appraisal from people, fittingly met with consistent performance on your part, will culminate in your leadership being seen as reliable.

The reliability rung on the ladder of leadership can be best attained if a leader can take cognizance of who people are. People are naturally scared of change, just as they are scared of being deceived or taken for granted. They want to trust you first before they can rely on you and your manifesto. They want to be sure you aren't going to remove all they've labored for or all they've been used to in a callous and thoughtless way. So there's need to first earn people's trust before their confidence can be achieved.

RELIABILITY BOOSTERS

There are four main qualities a leader must consistently exhibit before he can be said to have had a firm grip on the reliability rung of the leadership ladder.

Stability: This is easily proven in times of challenges and oppositions. A leader must be seen to be stable, even when the surrounding situations seem threatening or look scary. You don't want to show your heart on your face, as a leader. You must equip yourself with the strength to forge ahead and fail forward with the kind of trainings and preparations you must have put yourself through, as well as the quality of people you must have surrounded yourself with.

Whether you like it or not, questions will be thrown at your leadership and unforeseeable actions will be taken against you. But you must be prepared, at all times, to stand firm and stable on the purpose, vision and focus of your organization or calling. You cannot profess reliability when you fall at the appearance of storms. Almost half of Paul's ministerial life was spent in prison, but he was never deterred from his assignment. While as a prisoner, the administration of the churches he established was not held back. Instead, he always used the slightest opportunity he had to preach the gospel. In fact, despite all the troubles he encountered, his testimony was, "none of these things move me; nor do I count my life dear to myself, so that I may finish my race with joy..." (Acts 20:24). That is a stable leader right there!

An unstable leader, on the other hand, will be a bundle of frustration because of inability to cope with the vicissitudes of life. He will never be able to see opportunities in the adversities that he faces. All roads will seem like a dead-end end for him, leading him to being frustrated with himself and impatient with those around him.

Productivity: Literally, productivity is the rate at which goods are produced or the rate at which work is completed. It also means the quality or fact of generating, creating, or bringing forth goods and services. Productivity maximizes inputs to become exceptional outputs.

Naturally, people want to be successful in their endeavors. The same applies to leaders - they want to record optimal production of their goods and services for the benefits of all. To achieve this, smart leaders often find a way to make their employees work smarter rather than working harder. Bearing in mind that there is a physical limit to the number of working hours in a day, a good leader ensures that his team has the right tools, resources, and training to be effective and optimally productive.

One major way that a good leader inspires productivity in his followers is by analyzing everything that they do and eliminating tasks that add little or no value or detract from the actual goal. What makes a true leader is the ability to motivate his followers to be their best, while upholding the vision or mandate of the organization. When a team is adequately inspired and motivated, they are much more prepared to increase their output.

Let me refer to the leadership of Apostle Paul again. He proved himself to be an effective leader by not just being stable and reliable but also demonstrating productivity as can be seen from the numerous achievements he recorded in his lifetime. Even though he was not among the foundational disciples of Christ, he achieved much more than many of them in the expansion of the gospel. He wrote more than half of the New Testament Bible, while also establishing numerous churches from one part of the world to another.

Moreover, apart from enhancing productivity by leading by example (as demonstrated by Paul), a leader can also spur people under him to embrace better productivity through special recognitions of their efforts, giving out awards and paying compensations where necessary. This way, a leader not only ensures his continued productivity but also gets the active cooperation and participation of his subordinates, as well as the community.

Efficiency: Efficiency is the ability to do or produce something without wasting materials, time, or energy. It is the ability to accomplish a job with a minimum expenditure of time, efforts and resources.

Wastage is a major indicator of incompetence and a massive destroyer of integrity. It tarnishes the reliability reputation of a leader. Most times when a project is embarked upon and prematurely abandoned, a leader may forget, especially if it has become habitual; but the reality is that a lot of money, time and energy would have been wasted. It also creates a major moral burden because the revenue expended on such wasted ventures often comes from others, whether from tax-payers (for government projects) or tithes and offerings (for church people).

Sadly, wastage is something that is common in all segments of society, from country to country and organization to organization. Sometimes, a so-called leader, in a bid to project his own name or idea, simply abandons projects handed over by his predecessors and either starts his own or leaves the abandoned project to rot. This invariably gives room for misappropriation of scarce resources.

We have a very important lesson from the book of John concerning Jesus as an advocate of efficient leadership – that is, leadership without wastage. John 6:12-13 says, "So when they were filled, He said to His disciples, "Gather up the fragments that remain, so that nothing is lost." Therefore they gathered them up, and filled twelve baskets with the fragments of the five barley loaves which were left over by those who had eaten.

Isn't this instructive? Despite the fact that Jesus is the omnipotent Messiah who could do anything, including provision and multiplication of food, He instructed the disciples that no leftover of food from the feeding of the 5,000 people must be lost (other versions put it as "wasted").

By the way, out of all the gospel writers, only John deemed it fit to include this detail of why Jesus told the disciples to gather the leftover food. The reason is because he wants us to see and learn from the Master Himself about the importance of efficiency in all our endeavors. For any leader to have people's trust, inefficiency and waste – in terms of time management, utilization of resources and exertion of energy - must be totally discouraged among the team.

Consistency: Consistency could refer to application of accuracy; thickness or viscosity of liquid; or steadfast adherence to some principle. A good leader must practice and encourage consistency. This refers to consistency in everything good, noble and beneficial, regardless of the initiator.

Having said that, let's return to the issue of projects and ask ourselves: How consistent are today's leaders in following-up their predecessors' uncompleted projects? As I noted before, what we often find is that the incumbent simply discredits and discards the long-term project/policy like trash and then starts another similar project or policy. This is really common in the political sphere.

Take the case of the Obamacare healthcare Insurance policy in America, for instance. The project took close to four years to be conceptualized and another four years to be implemented. And then another leadership came into power to jettison the project and replace it with Trumpcare - simply because of nomenclature. So, I ask, where is consistency in government? Supposing another election ushers in a Bosede as president tomorrow, then we may start gearing up for the death of

Trumpcare and the rise of Bosedecare! This may sound funny but it's a seriously troubling trend.

Inconsistency is a terrible attribute that raises serious concerns about integrity. Leaders who are inconsistent can only earn the trust of people like them. Since they are not often true to their words, the majority of people often find it hard to trust them.

Yet, it is not only in political leadership that you find inconsistency. It rears its head in spiritual leadership and domestic leadership as well. There are "leaders" in ministry who cannot stick to their callings and convictions. They want to be anything and everything. In their church administration, anything goes. They lack the courage to resist negative influences, whether from within their congregations or from external sources. In the domestic setting, you find many spouses who are not consistent in their vows, commitments and decisions. They lack focus or direction. They are easily moved by what they see or hear. Every wind that blows redirects their minds. Naturally, they find it hard to give their offspring a stable upbringing.

Inconsistency in any area of life is a major turn-off for any rational follower or observer. Even God denounces inconsistency in His children. He says in Revelation 3:15-16, "I know your works, that you are neither cold nor hot. I could wish you were cold or hot. So then, because you are lukewarm, and neither cold nor hot, I will vomit you out of My mouth."

Once again, for a leader to be seen as reliable, all the above qualities must feature in his leadership style. For a leader to effectively make the most impact and leave the best legacies in a relationship, organization or community, all the above qualities must be harnessed. When this is achieved, it can be rightly said that another step of the leaders' ladder has been accomplished.

RESPONSIBILITY: THE TWIN OF RELIABILITY

As the above caption implies, responsibility is closely tied to reliability. The dictionary defines it as "a state, situation or fact of being answerable or accountable for something that's within one's power, control or management."

Personally, I will define responsibility as a

display of discipline to carry out an expected task and own the consequences thereof. For instance, responsibility is when a child is trained to clean, dust and tidy up his room or given a regular chore to complete, daily or weekly. Each time the child refuses to carry out these chores, he is reprimanded for his non-compliance or failure. This consequential condition makes the child to grow into the understanding that he is answerable and accountable for the completion of his chores; thus doing the chores or otherwise becomes his responsibility.

It so happens however that some trainings acquired in childhood are sometimes discarded on the way to adulthood. Many people grow up, throwing caution to the winds, acting without thinking – not knowing that they are putting their lives and those of others around them in jeopardy in the long run.

Sometimes, it is with this deficient orientation that many get into positions of leadership and, naturally, they demonstrate gross ignorance and ineptitude in performing their roles. It would be obvious to all around them that they lack understanding of how to handle situations of life. You find manifestations of this when an irresponsible man or woman goes into marriage, without considering what it means to BE in a marriage. There are also instances when people inherit their parents' wealth or take over their parents' organizations and become CEOs yet obviously lacking what it takes to maintain an empire or an inheritance.

This is the exact reason many organizations – whether secular or religious – are collapsing. It's simply because the leaders do not possess knowledge of what is expected of them or what to do with the people within their sphere of influence. Forgetting that the passion to accomplish tangible result, regardless of circumstances, is a key component of responsibility, they prefer to spend their time giving excuses.

It is a great waste when a leader in any segment of the society proves to be irresponsible. Lots of resources are wasted or left to rot. It is comparable to the waste incurred by the prodigal son when he squandered the inheritance given to him by his father (Luke 15:11-32). Thank God, he had a forgiving father to run back to.

I need to add here that responsibility goes beyond completing a task and accepting the consequences. It also entails owning up to one's wrong decisions and mistakes. Responsibility avoids the blame-game or pointing an accusing finger to someone else when a mistake or misconduct is noticed.

Naturally we don't want to be seen at the point of our weakness or found guilty in the area of our struggle. Yet, I do not see anything wrong in admitting a fault or misconduct, showing remorse and tendering necessary apologies. The problem is that some leaders have this mindset that they are above reprimanding. They think they have attained a level where "sorry" or "I apologize" is not expected of them. What they do instead is try to use their authority to thwart responsibility.

Indeed, the world would be a better place for all to live peacefully when spouses easily take responsibility for the consequences of falling into adultery, rather than shifting it to cultural tendencies; when CEOs are ready to apologize for flouting organizational policies, and make amends; when political leaders understand that great power goes hand-in-hand with great responsibility - towards the people they are governing and the world at large.

In sum, the reliability/responsibility rung on the leadership ladder can significantly determine the fate and legacies of a leader. In other words, it is a two-edged sword that if taken care of and adhered to will not only foster vibrancy, dignity and honor in the leader's ladder, but will also build the foundation for a healthy society, lively workplaces and conquering congregations.

Chapter 3

E - ENCOURAGEMENT

"When you encourage others, you, in the process, are encouraged because you're making a commitment and difference in that person's life. Encouragement really does make a difference." ~ Zig Ziglar

This chapter is very dear to my heart because the issue discussed here has helped me to be more positive towards life and its affairs. It has built me up to see people through the lens of positivity until they prove otherwise. Essentially, this trait of maturity, has helped me to see others through the eyes of God.

Merriam-Webster defines "encourage" thus:

- To inspire with courage, spirit, or hope
- To attempt to persuade

- To spur on, to stimulate into doing something

- To give help or patronage to foster

Zig Ziglar has rightly simplified encouragement to be a dual and reciprocal process. Encouraging others makes you to be encouraged. James M. Barrie puts it this way, "Those who bring sunshine into the lives of others, cannot keep it from themselves." However, the reverse is also true – when you choose to cause frustration and discouragement for others, you will sooner or later find yourself in the same murky mire.

Moreover, a careful analysis will reveal that the words "encourage" and "courage" are related because they both have to do with the HEART. That is, both have to do with states of mind. A leader has to demonstrate largeness of heart before he can be called an encourager. Since leaders lead people and not objects, a caring heart is a must for them.

The world is filled with so much negativity that poisons motivation and effectively wearies the hearts of people from achieving greatness or triggering progress in the world around them. We all sometimes need someone to scream or whisper into our eardrums, as the case may be: "YOU CAN DO IT".

An encouraging leader boosts self-confidence, spurs performance, and cures the soul of sickness. He allows others to have a say, and makes them to have the feeling of "we are in this together", which further enhances commitment to improved performance and increased output.

HOME LESSON

This reminds me of one of my children, whose walking stage took her almost one year. She could grab on edges of furniture but could not just shift her legs to move. Any attempt to help shift or move her legs often made her to burst into tears and simply sit back down.

To help the situation, my husband and I devised some ways to encourage her to not feel being pushed to do what she was afraid to do. We created an atmosphere of love and acceptance; making her know that someone was there to help her from falling. We usually sang and clapped when she was in standing position (she loved songs with her name in them). Naturally she would want to sit down to dance to the rhythms, but I quickly got in the way to prevent her from sitting and also let her know that she could dance while standing.

Gradually this got her into shifting one leg at a time while dancing. Before long, the shifting of one dancing leg developed to two dancing legs, which later got her to walk. She actually walked off all the arrears of "fear of walking" in one week!

ENCOURAGEMENT TIPS

This is the same approach expected of every leader - to encourage people in the area of their gifting towards achieving the goal and purpose of being together. Most times we think leadership means lounging in in a gilded chair in a giant office, giving a string of commands to subordinates. No, that is not it. We are in that leadership position because God allows it and people approve of it. Therefore, our responsibility and accountability must be towards both – God and man.

As an acronym, the word TEAM means Together, Each Achieves More. Since this is a fact, then leaders need to ascribe the success of their organizations to the performance of all. In addition to this, there are a few more strategies that leaders can use to encourage their followers and subordinates.

Successes must be recognized, appreciated and celebrated. This creates a sense of belonging in the team, which will further enhance them to do more and have the interest of the organization in mind. I call this positive reinforcement. However, it is not only successes and achievements that must be recognized – every positive effort made in the direction of success must be recognized and commended to encourage continuity.

Enthusiastically re-echo the vision and objectives of being together on a regular basis. This is emphasized because human beings are sometimes forgetful – due to pressures of life – and thus easy to be distracted from pursuing and achieving set goals. Forgetfulness and distractions are more common when manipulation and enticements are at play. But when you, as a leader, repeatedly highlight the collective vision, it makes people to be focused. This also drives away indolence, making goals to be accomplished faster.

Create a healthy, conducive and comfortable

working environment. This motivates, encourages and boosts productivity in a spectacular way. I know of an organization that provides free work-out sessions at beak time for their employees. I also know of a church that provided free tickets for their congregation to watch movies at the theater. Such gestures make people to know that their interests are part of the growth of the organization.

Be a die-hard optimist and morale booster. Ensure to constantly express confidence in the team and be positive that goals, which might look impossible ordinarily, can be achieved where there is an encouraged team. Confidence in the team will definitely give room for innovative ideas.

Encourage constant training (or lifelong learning). This is emphasized because of the nature of man. Where there are frequent trainings, success is inevitable, and higher output is achieved with ease. Trainings must be on-going and must add value to the team.

INTRAPERSONAL ENCOURAGEMENT
It is imperative to state, at this point, that

encouragement is not only interpersonal or relational but also intrapersonal. This is when the focus of encouragement is on the leader himself. There are times when things and situations seem so tough and all efforts to manage them seem to be failing; there are times when inputs are far greater than outputs, when the backdoor exit gets wider by the day, while the front door remains practically closed. This is when then the leader has to make some personal decisions before things totally fall apart. The first decision is to positively encourage himself. This will help him to regain his strength and the confidence that he can make it, he can move forward and he can still achieve greatness. Regardless of circumstances or the attitude of people all around, you don't give up or look down on yourself or your vision and dreams.

Intrapersonal encouragement will propel you into some resolutions and actions that can light up the flame of enthusiasm again. Thomas Edison experienced the power of intrapersonal encouragement when trying to invent the electric bulb. Hundreds of times he failed but he refused to give up. What kept him going, despite repeated jibes and discouraging attitudes from people around him? The knowledge that he was gaining valuable experience from his failures. Thus, when he was pressured from within and without to stop his experiments, he kept saying: "I have not failed. I've just found hundreds of ways that won't work." And of course, as he kept trying, he found the perfect formula with which he achieved his goal.

That's the attitude of a leader right there. You don't quit because of failures; nor should you be moved by the negative opinions of people – including your followers. They are not the ones leading, you are. They are not the visionaries, you are. So, then, you don't just give up or throw in the towel. The classic example that I like to cite for this model of leadership is that of David in 1 Samuel 30. He and his band of soldiers had gone for a battle, leaving their families and belongings behind in the city given to them. When they returned from the battle, what they saw was massive catastrophe: "So David and his men came to the city, and there it was, burned with fire; and their wives, their sons, and their daughters had been taken captive. Then David and the people who were with him lifted up their voices and wept, until they had no more power to weep. And David's two wives, Ahinoam the Jezreelitess, and Abigail the widow of Nabal the Carmelite, had been taken captive. Now David was greatly distressed, for the people spoke of stoning him, because the soul of all the people was grieved, every man for his sons and his daughters..." (3-6).

I don't know of an experience that can be more devastating for a leader as this. It's one thing to lose all of your assets and investments, it's another to have your followers and subordinates losing respect for you and calling you a total failure. Of course, David, being human, wept and was distressed at the loss of family, properties and dignity – but he did something that every leader must learn to do. The concluding part of verse 6 says, "But David strengthened [encouraged] himself in the Lord his God."

That is intrapersonal encouragement right there – which indeed is the best and most effective form of motivation any leader could have. In the case of David, because of this resolve to encourage himself, he was able to recover all he had lost, including the respect and loyalty of his followers.

Encouragement is likened to the fuel and the power source in a car, without which a car cannot move. When a leader is not an encourager, the establishment is heading towards a standstill. No man will want to put all his mind and efforts into a venture when he realizes that the man at the helm of affairs is a slave-driver. Beyond this however is that, as an encourager pours his fuel of encouragement into his employees and people around him, he too must encourage himself to move up on the leader's ladder of progress and success.

As a last line in this chapter, I need to point out something about encouragement in this digital age. I shared with someone sometimes ago, the need to be more mindful of what we share on our social media platforms. The world is already heavily burdened with stories of woes and wars. Moral decadence is at its peak and social values have been drastically eroded. However, we can make up our minds not to contribute to the dismal picture of our world. Our individual consciousness of what we post and share can gradually effect powerful changes in people's thinking and perceptions. We should thus be more concerned about sharing messages of hope, encouragement and empowerment; rather than those of doom and distress.

Chapter 4

A - AUTHENTICITY AND ACCOUNTABILITY

"A 'NO' uttered from the deepest conviction is better than a 'YES' merely uttered to please, or worse, to avoid trouble". ~ Mahatma Gandhi

This stage of the leader's ladder is a bit thorny and thus can be described as a road less frequently traveled. Yet, if given careful attention, it can become the leader's most powerful catalyst for greatness.

Let me begin by asking, who is that leader that is real to the core? Who is that leader that, having attained the place of power and authority, will not discard or compromise his campaign promises? We have become used to the mindset that "no man is perfect" – and this is what accounts for the general mistrust that characterizes the relationship between the leaders and the led in our society.

THE BASICS

Authenticity in leadership is more of who you are and what you stand for. It comes from inside of you, deeply rooted and unaffected by external pressures. No super-power or cabal can hijack or militate against who you really are.

Authenticity speaks of genuineness, trustworthiness, faithfulness, dependability, integrity and other similar virtues. People generally expect a leader to be exemplary and exceptional – or at least to be the best of the pack – especially in the area of morality and trustworthiness. The way many followers view those in leadership can be compared to the way people view a document that comes with an embossed seal or logo - there's always a sense of reverence, acceptance and credibility attached to it.

Unfortunately, when it comes to leadership it has been proven again and again that a book can't be adjudged to be good just by the pleasantness of its cover. And this is why many followers are often disappointed in leadership. Imagine having an orange, or what you think is an orange. With your knife in one hand, you are ready to peel and tuck into your orange. But as soon as you peel off the first slice of rind, you discover that instead of having a juicy orange, what you have is an avocado. Apparently, you will be disappointed, devastated, disgusted and probably scared almost at the same time! This is the state of mind that many leaders subject their people to through lack of authenticity.

We leaders expect our followers to give up their time, intellect, gift and net worth in exchange for the outcome of a vision or dream that we dangle before them. Yet, a short way down the road, we detour into the alley of falsehood, fakery, manipulation and callousness, forgetting that we had most likely begged for the consent and approval of the same people at the beginning of the journey.

DEEPER ISSUE

Using the above illustration, it's even possible that you are originally an avocado, but for you to be accepted, nominated or approved, you "covered up" with an orange peel - forgetting that you would be exposed by and by. Fullness of time will always bring out who you really are.

What this means is that a leader cannot thrive or succeed if his leadership is built on the faulty foundation of falsehood. Especially in this age of social media, the world has become so advanced in communication technology that it doesn't take too long for someone's dirty linen to be seen and exposed. So why do we need cover-ups? Why can't we try to be real? Why can't our yea be yea and our nay be nay?

There is really no compulsion in leadership to warrant employing the weapon of deception. We all can lead in our respective spheres of influence without compromising leadership principles. Therefore, why is it so difficult for us to handle our weaknesses without cover ups? Why are we handling our struggles in such a way that when its traces come out, we want to commit suicide?

Really, you don't need the approval of people to live your life. You don't have to be like some leaders whose focus is to be "people's person" all the time. They always want to satisfy others at the expense of their lives, homes and future.

They forget that leaders are firstly, humans, before their leadership roles.

Yes, we all are humans! So, defend your beliefs. Your inner-man or what you stand for should not be masked to the point of not knowing when you're becoming a manipulator. You need not pretend in order to please anybody. If there is any area you think you are deficient, all you need do is to seek ways to make amendments, improve on yourself and move forward.

It must be said though that for some leaders their problem is admitting that they need to work on themselves for necessary improvements. To make amendments and corrections is so hard for such leaders. Unfortunately, they only succeed in sending away their help and support systems. Self-deception and manipulative approach to issues of life don't work on the leader's ladder.

QUEST FOR AUTHENTIC LEADERSHIP

In 2013, I convened a seminar for "Lily Girlz" (the youth section of a womanhood organization), The seminar was given the theme, "Be Authentic". The goal was to teach and empower the youths on the significance of wholeness and real living in a polluted world, as well as how to identify the seductive factors that can lead them into an inauthentic life. The seminar was well acclaimed because of the fruits and post conference testimonies that were received.

If we are to be authentic as leaders and thrive on the leader's ladder, we need not only constantly declare what we stand for, but also demonstrate our real character along with our visions. An authentic leader will not be found in the "do what I say, don't do what I do" community. These are the people whose pronouncements are different from the character they project on the outside.

It is unfortunate that many of us easily forget that the leadership platform is primarily meant to help others and molding them into being successful leaders themselves. What most of us concern ourselves with are authority and power. This I see as a symptom of lack of vision or misplacement of priorities, which is mostly found in those who see leadership as an avenue to usurp power and create errands for people.

This reminds me of what a contributor said during a leadership seminar I convened for church leaders in June 2017. The person disclosed that the major causes of failure for most leaders, especially religious leaders, are lack of focus and lack of understanding of the position they occupy. He cited the example of a spirit-filled teacher of the word, who apparently because of lack of understanding of the place of a teacher in ministry, went ahead to start his own church and declared himself a prophet and an apostle. Of course, it is just a matter of time before such a confused person will lead his entire congregation astray. It is no wonder that respect and honor for people of God continue to diminish daily, thus making the devil to succeed in gaining more souls into 'its' kingdom. No wonder that topics from the word of God are daily subjected to controversies!

Gone are the days when people worshipped God "in truth and in spirit"; it is gradually being turned to "worship God with an open mind and logic". I pray that the standard of God's word will be raised forever in our churches.

But it is not only religious establishments that are guilty of not staying true to their calling; lots of secular and corporate organizations also do same. An example is a tax preparer outfit that also serves as a real estate agent, loan officer, insurance agent, car dealership agent, and money transfer agent. The question is what is the focus of this outfit?

SIGNPOSTS OF AUTHENTICITY

Listed below are the five keys to identifying authentic leaders:

- They identify who they are and hold their integrity in high esteem.

- They are very thoughtful of their vision alongside the people around them.

- They are real and find it difficult to camouflage their feelings.

- They are able to express their emotions freely and clearly without being judgmental.

- They are open to learn from their mistakes without bitterness.

If behind what a person says and does is a defensive and self-deceptive approach to life, then no matter how passionate and committed they are to a cause, ultimately, they are neither being true to themselves nor the people that follow them.

ACCOUNTABILITY

This is a word that is often interchanged with "responsibility" and if not clearly differentiated, can be taken to mean the same thing. Responsibility is the expectation of people from a leader, while accountability is the willingness of a leader to accept responsibility.

Accountability is not only about what we do or do not do, but taking responsibility for the actions of our team-members and subordinates. Accountability specifically relates to the obligation of an individual or organization to account for activities, accept responsibility for them, and then disclose the results in a transparent manner. The key words in this definition are the highlighted ones, which are often found to be missing in the ladders of many present-day leaders.

There are leaders who accept the responsibility for activities related to their offices but fail to give adequate report and feedback on such activities. Many leaders quickly easily forget that the power they have was entrusted to them by the people. This is why many don't see the need for reports or think that they can present haphazard reports that lack transparency, especially when it comes to personal misconduct and financial situations.

A survey of some thriving organizations shows that they are able to retain the support and loyalty of their shareholders through their timely and regular financial reports. This not only communicates integrity on the part of the executives but also gives the shareholders a sense of belonging in the growth of such organizations.

Unfortunately, this practice is lacking in many of our companies, worship centers, communities and governmental institutions. Sometimes you find CEOs declaring that they own their companies and can run it anyhow they like. You equally see religious organizations finding it difficult to render financial reports annually (if not quarterly) to their congregations, because they probably don't see any need for it. In other words, they don't see the need for accountability.

THE ACCOUNTABILITY PARTNER

One essential element that is missing in the accountability rung of the ladders of many leaders is the accountability partner. The accountability partner serves as a monitor or mentor to help someone keep to their commitments. He's like a trainer that seeks the success of the other. The scripture clearly states that: "As iron sharpens iron, so a man sharpens the countenance of his friend" (Proverbs 27:17).

As previously mentioned, accountability transcends one's activities; it extends to the actions of delegated subordinates. For instance, when a registered nurse delegates collection of vital signs for a patient to a CNA (clinical nursing assistant), that registered nurse is accountable for the responsibility of that CNA, as well as for the consequential changes in status of the patient as it relates to the vital signs brought by the CNA. Thus, the nurse may jeopardize his career if he totally relies on the judgment of the CNA to administer treatment on the patient. Similarly, in an organization, if an executive gives a staff a responsibility, the executive should not only see to the completion of the task, but be familiar with the outcome of the task through follow-up. There is no alternative to this. As a writer rightly says, "Leaders who fail to appreciate this fundamental precept of accountability must also fail to master the profound commitment true leadership demands".

Chapter 5

D - DELEGATION

"Surround yourself with the best people you can find, delegate authority, and don't interfere as long as the policy you've decided upon is being carried out"
~ *Ronald Reagan*

Having been jolted from an unplanned nap, I immediately noticed that I had slept for two hours on my couch, leaving me with just three hours more to do my one-hour homecare visit (as a nurse), as well as complete food preparation for the women's biweekly meeting I was hosting. With this limited time frame, I had to quickly get the recipe ready and provided a step by step instruction for my daughter on how to complete the meal. I delegated dusting and space set-up to my son, while I dashed out to my client's home for the home care nursing visit. On getting back home, I was so surprised to have a very delicious meal already prepared, and the meal table had been neatly set before the first guest came in.

This is what delegation of assignments can do. Not only did it speed up my schedule but the touch of finesse and expertise that was used was beyond my imagination. This is a way to get things done faster by others. Ultimately, my children were not only happy to be part of the success of the meeting, but were very proud to flaunt their expertise on food and venue preparation. I call this having a sense of belonging.

UNDERSTANDING DELEGATION

The Merriam Webster dictionary defines delegation as:

"The act of transferring of responsibility for the performance of an activity from one individual to another while retaining accountability for the outcome."

"Directing the performance of one or more people to accomplish organizational goals."

This is a leadership skill that cuts across all segments of life. It is indispensable in the home environment as much as in the workplace, the community and the church. To succeed in life, you need people to work with; you cannot succeed in isolation. An organization cannot succeed when tasks and outputs are robed around the leader. As a matter of fact, your success and creation of legacy is determined by the number of people you are connected to and are able to work with. As Stephen Covey has rightly observed, "People and organization don't grow much without delegation and completed staff work because they are confined to the capacities of the boss and reflect both personal strength and weaknesses."

Apparently, any leader who's scared to shed some of his authority to his subordinates is not fit to be called a leader, because he lacks trust. He is either phobic or having serious complex issues. The effect of that on an organization is stunted growth, as the workers are severely impeded from growing or from moving the company to the next level. This will eventually cause the organization to die.

This strategy of delegation is highly needed in our religious and political organizations for progress and success to be achieved. Presently, for whatever reasons, many pulpits and CEO tables cannot be shared or delegated to "next in rank" subordinates. What is prevalent is "If not the leader, it has to be one of the children". And when it's time for the whole family to go on vacation, which they rarely do, then the problem of who handles events will ensue.

Remember that everyone is called but few are chosen. The fact that you are among the "chosen" to lead is an opportunity to justify the privilege conferred on you through a systematic and strategic team selection. Your impacts and contributions can be further distributed and multiplied through the efforts of your team, thus creating bigger room to build an outlasting legacy.

LEARNING FROM THE PACESETTER

If delegation were unimportant, Jesus, our Lord and pacesetter, would not have chosen disciples to work with Him. He painstakingly selected these men, breathed His power and poured His teachings into them, and later delegated them to go and do for others what they had seen Him do among them.

Mind you, Jesus didn't send the disciples out empty, but with instructions and blessings. Mark 6:7-9 says, "And He called the twelve to Himself, and began to send them out two by two, and gave them power over unclean spirits. He commanded them to take nothing for the journey except a staff—no bag, no bread, no copper in their money belts— but to wear sandals, and not to put on two tunics."

Jesus gave room for practicality. He allowed them to rejoice in their little and petty faith, but He further taught them and gave them more instructions. These are the expectations in delegation which leaders have to be conversant with.

If Steven Paul Jobs, the late American entrepreneur, business magnate, inventor and chairman, chief executive officer, and co-founder of Apple Inc. had robed the multibillion-dollar conglomerate around himself (the "me, myself and I" syndrome), without allowing innovators on board, the organization would have died along with him by now.

DIVIDENDS OF DELEGATION

Delegation is not in any way removing your headship, authority, accountability or focus from the original vision; it rather refreshes and strengthens you, while easing some burdens off your shoulders. Besides, delegation is just something you cannot avoid if you must succeed as a leader. As Anthea Turner put it, "The first rule of management is DELEGATION. Don't try and do everything because you can't."

Delegating authority motivates employees, facilitates efficiency and eliminates time wastage. It also improves people's morale, boosts team spirit and enhances cordial relationship within the organization which further advances the company's success and accomplishments.

10 CHECKLIST PRINCIPLES FOR DELEGATION

1. I am the vision-carrier, whose gifts are for a legacy and not for a cubicle.

2. I have my strengths and weaknesses as a human being.

3. I must diligently and prayerfully select and know my team.

4. I must create time to add value to them and celebrate their uniqueness.

5. I must align the vision, objectives and goals of my organization as the teams' platform.

6. I realize that delegation is about the growth of the vision, and thus allow for refinements and innovations.

7. I will show, teach, encourage and display the sequence and process of achieving the ultimate goal to my subordinates.

8. We all are determined to embark and collaborate on projects as a workforce.

9. I allow my team to execute projects within a reasonable time frame while I watch and evaluate with dignity.

10. I give room to applaud results and reinforce continuity and diversity.

Can you see that there is a thin line that links these principles together? Did you notice that the starting point is from the CEO or managing director, as the case may be? Did you notice that he is still the person in the last stage to append his signature for the project's execution? Even when you think he is out of the scene and invisible, he is still either monitoring or working on other researches. In the end, the risks and dividends are shared proportionally.

On the whole, the success of delegation is best determined when everyone involved is happy for achieving success or learns why the team failed. If this is practicable in private enterprises, why does it appear impracticable among national leaders, especially those in third world countries? The answer is not farfetched.

Delegation is a principle of success and development. And as it was stated at the beginning of this book, principles should neither be skipped nor allowed to work in isolation without knitting each level together. Unfortunately, the leaders in many third world countries do not even believe in principles; they instead greedily devise their own paradigms of operation and evaluation. No wonder the dividends are shared by just few in the top positions, while the risks are thrown down to the populace. The brunt of their leadership failure is sent down the ladder for the commoners to live with.

Chapter 6

TO LEAD IS TO R-E-A-D

"Not all readers are leaders, but all leaders are readers."
~Harry S. Truman

Now that we have dissected the various interconnecting components (or rungs) of our leadership ladder, we have to bring the different parts together again, so we can look at the whole picture.

In my few strides into leadership operations, I have discovered that many people that are yearning, thriving or longing to maximize their leadership skills are "falling backward", as against "falling forward" – thereby making the same mistakes of their predecessors. I used the word "falling" just to denote the erroneous feeling we subject ourselves to when we make a mistake, or when we are overtaken by errors. We must know that as leaders, we are, first, human beings. This means that we are bound to err once in a while; we are bound to make mistakes, or act in some ways that will disappoint our mentees. But we don't crawl back into oblivion and wrap ourselves up in the cocoon of regrets. No, we get back up, make amends, learn from our faults, determine never to repeat them, and thereafter forge ahead.

HEART OF THE MATTER

The reason there is unending "falling backward" in most of our leadership practice is because we have not been keeping to the principles of R-E-A-D, as already discussed in the previous chapters. I believe that things will change, from all we have been exposed to. But as I said, we need to look at the whole picture here.

R-E-A-D literally means what it says, READ! It is an action word, a verb, which means that it involves doing something. We can define it as the act of looking at and comprehending the meaning of a written material or printed matter by mentally interpreting the characters or symbols of which it is composed.

I like the way Merriam-Webster puts it: to receive or take in the sense of (letters, symbols, etc.) especially by sight or touch to study the movements of, with mental formulation of the communication expressed in books to learn from what one has seen or found in writing or printing to become acquainted with or look over the contents of (something, such as a book).

These literal definitions are very explicit; they nail down the points I wanted to amplify. Many of us in leadership show ourselves off to be learned, but still operate in a box. How many of us can boast of purposefully going to a bookstore to buy a book to READ? Or going online with the intention of reading contents that will add value to us and our ministries or organization?

Many of us would rather spend hours reading news of fear and woes, under the guise of "I need to know what is going on around me." My mentor once said that he'd rather spend two hours of his time with a pen and paper, writing up eight pages of edifying material, than flipping through pages of social media that will not add value to his ministry but instead infect his spirit being and make him to be added to the census of garbage-mongers.

There are leaders who have tons of books on their shelves that are gathering dust, year-in-year-out – books that were bought with money, but left to decorate the shelves. Many don't read because they think they can adjudge the content of a book by the design of the cover or by the name of the writer or publisher.

A PECULIAR OBSERVATION

Sorry to say, but I have found that this tendency towards apathy to books seems to be more common with us, black folks. A writer once declared that if you want to keep a treasure from a black man, put it in a book and give the book to him for safe keep. He will keep it to the end of the day without opening it to discover the treasure. This sounded uncomplimentary to me for many years, until a time I had the opportunity to lead a group of leaders. A peculiar incident that needed intervention was the prevailing topic at that time. So, among other Christmas/New Year gifts I wrapped for each of these leaders, was a 54-page book, with a cover title that resonated with was going on. To my amazement, after five weeks, I made reference to some points in the book and, alas, their countenances' and gestures spoke volumes of their unfamiliarity with the contents of the book. In fact, it was as if I was referring to a book that was yet to be published.

The excuses the leaders gave for not reading the book were unlimited - from lack of time, to too many pressures from kids, to job issues and so on. I realized therefore that if I had indeed hidden a treasure in any of the books, none of the leaders would have seen or noticed it.

How many leaders really take reading as a hobby? This is why many leaders often base their thinking, ideas and operations solely on the shallow expressions of "they say" or "I heard someone (name) say". They rarely have facts to base their operations on. Instead, they rely on the "fire brigade" approach to deal with issues. And naturally, they are usually short-sighted in their approaches.

JOYS OF READING

Among the many benefits that I have gained from reading wide, some are listed below to encourage the readers of this book:

1. Reading helps to reduce stress, as the hours you spend reading give less time for frivolities.

2. Your mental faculty is stimulated to revolve round the storyline of the book you are reading, which thus improves your general knowledge and expands your vocabulary.

3. You are able to develop the ability to focus and concentrate, since quality reading engages the whole of your being.

4. Reading makes you have wider perspectives on situations and events. Consequently, your analytical thinking skills become comparatively stronger.

The bottom-line is that a leader must be a reader. If you want to lead well, you must read well and wide. Read from people that have been there before you, know their pitfalls and their strengths, know how they overcame; let their experience boost your own expertise. Let their shortcomings be your long-term gain.

SOME SELF-ASSESSMENT

As I wrap up the message of this book, I

believe it is necessary to do some introspection. Where do you belong in your leadership ladder? Considering all we have examined in all the chapters up to this point, can you say you are a true leader or space-filler, without full understanding of the requirements of the position you are occupying?

Space-filler leaders only position themselves for endless struggle and they never last. You need to be versed, mature and conversant with the demands of that position you are occupying. So many are the instances when political leaders attain offices they don't merit, just because they belong to the popular political party or popular family. Leadership is not about space-filling or someone sitting at the head of the table. You can have the space, but what has been poured into the space or inherent in the space matters?

Genesis 13:1-18 tells us the grace Abraham carried that earned him the credibility of being a friend to God. Apparently, the anointing that Abraham had was far greater than what Lot could have envisaged. They were both leaders in their own rights but wouldn't there have been a better ending to the story of their relationships, if Lot had given total deference to Abraham to choose a suitable land for him? Or, at least, allow Abraham to choose first, being the older one?

Abraham's position presupposes that of a mentor, a leader whom Lot should always owe allegiance to. Now, what does a mentor do? A mentor pours grace and fills up into your weaknesses. Moses poured grace into Joshua and he inherently achieved what Moses could not achieve.

Are you designated and raised to a leadership position based on your gifts and demeanor, but lacking any of the components of the leader's ladder in your life and operation? Or maybe you are probably struggling with your authenticity (realness) or reliability and responsibility rungs. It is never too late to pick up the pieces because leadership is not a vacuum or reservoir but a channel.

Leadership is not about head knowledge; it's about how much you are channeling and how many are channeled through you. Gehazi in 2 kings 5:20-27 had some qualities that awarded him the privilege to be working for Elisha; yet he displayed zero reliability through the sins of covetousness and lying when he went back to Namaan, the leper. So also was Judas Iscariot, Jesus' disciple, whose stealing and greediness made him to trade his master for money. Unsurprisingly, the end of these two men was miserable.

If as a leader you are struggling with some challenges, it is advisable not to cover up. Go for counseling and support from those in higher authority. And in case you have simply imposed, manipulated or forced your way into leadership, it is not too late to make amends, especially as stories of impostors always end in shame and regrets. Struggling will always be their experience. It was the case with Jacob when he connived with his mother to manipulatively Isaac and rob Esau, his brother, of his birthright (Genesis 25). Jacob would later get his comeuppance of deceit at Laban's house. Genesis 29 and 30 provide glaring details on this. There is also the case of David's son, Adonijah, who super-imposed himself as the king while his father was still alive. His end was with shame and ridicule (1 Kings 1 and 2). All these are to serve as examples so we don't fall into the same error.

CONCLUSION

We have come to the realization that any given society if well-managed by a competent and knowledgeable leader can become tremendously transformed. On the other hand, a retrogressive, half-baked and inside-the-box leader has nothing to offer but crises and chaos.

Literally 'R-E-A-D(ing)', shows that a leader is widely read and ripe to lead. He knows or has gone through history to see the strengths and weaknesses of past leaders and is ready to bring innovation and landmark achievements to the office he is occupying. In essence, a good leader must be a great reader. You don't lead with a boxed knowledge.

Hypothetically, 'R-E-A-D(ing)' is a pointer to the character of a visionary leader. Inasmuch as his dealings are focused and centered on people, his character should be humane both inside and outside. A combination of these two will surely make his grip on the ladder of success to be firmly rooted and his rise will be phenomenal.

Usually, many think that when they get to the top, they will have more time to read; whereas it is your reading aptitude that will not only make ways for you at the top but will help you to stay at the top, because it is what you know, that you will give. If you don't earn knowledge by creating time to be a good reader, then you have nothing to offer to be a great leader. Kelsey Meyer once said, "If you are a leader, you should be striving to develop knowledge to improve yourself, your company, and the people who work for you. To do anything less is to shortchange your ability to lead".

Then if this ladder of R.E.A.D is fully adhered to, we will not only see a vibrant, homely and paradise-on-earth society, but live in it. The leadership of R.E.A.D is powerful and it is needed for our organizations, communities, our countries to overcome retrogression and waste of resources.

ABOUT BOSEDE ADETUNJI

Bosede Adetunji is a Life, Spiritual and Leadership Coach, Pastor & Motivational Speaker that empowers Womanhood and Organizations to fulfill their Purpose, create paths to their Breakthroughs and Amplify their Success.

As a result of the Coaching, Teaching & Speaking programs that she does for Secular and Religious Outfits; Redemptive and Restoration of lives, Homes and Relationships have been achieved and maintained.

Her decades of passion for Womanhood and experience in Leadership formation of Christ Harvest Church, Ohio & "The Esteemed Woman" #lilyinhishands organization, have made many youth girls reconciled back to their parents, marriages have been restored and gifts (talents) have been discovered and celebrated.

Being equipped to offer workshops, seminars, keynote speaking and coaching, to aid Personal, Professional and Organizational growth, She, will support you through achieving your goals and succeed now.

Holds BSc in Mass Communication, major in Public Relations. Leadership Coaching Certification from John C. Maxwell & Life Coaching Certification from Life Training Institute. She is happily married with biological and spiritual children.

NOTE

NOTE

_____

_____

_____

_____

_____

_____

_____

_____

_____

_____

_____

_____

NOTE

_____

_____

_____

_____

_____

_____

_____

_____

_____

_____

_____

_____

_____

NOTE

NOTE

NOTE